KERI DAVIES

Who's Who in
The
Archers

2009

For Tim and Ruth.

3 5 7 9 10 8 6 4 2

This book is published to accompany the BBC Radio 4 serial *The Archers*.
The editor of *The Archers* is Vanessa Whitburn.

Published in 2008 by BBC Books, an imprint of Ebury Publishing.
Ebury Publishing is a division of the Random House Group Ltd.

The Random House Group Limited Reg. No. 954009.
Addresses for companies within the Random House Group can be found
at www.randomhouse.co.uk

A CIP catalogue record for this book is available from the British Library.

ISBN 978 1 846 07579 7

The Random House Group Limited supports The Forest Stewardship
Council (FSC), the leading international forest certification organisation.
All our titles that are printed on Greenpeace approved FSC certified paper
carry the FSC logo. Our paper procurement policy can be found at
www.rbooks.co.uk/environment

 Mixed Sources
Product group from well-managed
forests and other controlled sources
www.fsc.org Cert no. TT-COC-2139
FSC © 1996 Forest Stewardship Council

Commissioning editor: Albert DePetrillo
Project editors: Steve Tribe and Kari Speers
Typeset in Garamond Light
Printed and bound in Great Britain by CPI Mackays, Chatham ME5 8TD

To buy books by your favourite authors and register for offers,
visit www.rbooks.co.uk

Events in Ambridge are constantly changing, but we have done our
best to make *Who's Who in The Archers 2009* accurate at the time of
publication.

Official Archers Website: bbc.co.uk/archers, to listen again to *Archers*
episodes, including podcasts and an audio archive of the last seven days.
The site also features daily plot synopses, news, information, a map of
Ambridge, a detailed timeline, archive moments, quizzes and chat.

Official Fan Club: Archers Addicts
01789 207480 www.archers-addicts.com

THE AUTHOR
Having spent the early part of his life flitting between jobs as varied
as writing advertising copy to serving in the RAF, Keri Davies found
lasting happiness in Ambridge in 1991. A former senior producer for
the programme, he is currently an Archers scriptwriter and runs the
programme's official website.

WELCOME TO AMBRIDGE

W e're delighted that our handy guide to the characters and locations in *The Archers* has reached its tenth edition.

The book takes into account another exciting year in Ambridge, including Alan and Usha's controversial marriage, the effects of TB in Oliver Sterling's herd and the new baby – indeed the new building – at Willow Farm.

We hope you enjoy getting up to date – and we hope you like the new look.

Vanessa Whitburn
Editor, *The Archers*

FREQUENTLY ASKED QUESTIONS

When and how can I hear the programme?

On BBC Radio 4 (92–95 FM, 198 LW and on digital radio and television). Transmission times: 7pm Sunday to Friday, repeated at 2pm the next day, excluding Saturdays. An omnibus edition of the whole week's episodes is broadcast every Sunday at 10am. It can also be heard worldwide via podcasts or the BBC iPlayer (go to the *Archers* website: bbc.co.uk/archers).

How many people listen?

Nearly five million every week in the UK alone. *The Archers* is the most popular non-news programme on BBC Radio 4, and the most-listened-to BBC programme online.

How long has it been going?

Five pilot episodes were broadcast on the BBC Midlands Home Service in Whit Week 1950, but *The Archers*' first national broadcast was on 1 January 1951. Episode 15,674, broadcast on 1 January 2009, makes this comfortably the world's longest-running radio drama.

How did it start?

The creator of *The Archers*, Godfrey Bascley, devised the programme as a means of educating farmers in modern production methods when Britain was still subject to food rationing.

So it's an educational programme?

Not any more. *The Archers* lost its original educational remit in the early 1970s – but it still prides itself on the quality of its research and its reflection of real rural life.

How is it planned and written?

The Editor, Vanessa Whitburn, leads a ten-strong production team and nine writers as they plot the complicated lives of the families in Ambridge, looking ahead months or sometimes years in biannual long-term meetings. The detailed planning is done at monthly script meetings about two months ahead of transmission. Each writer produces a week's worth of scripts in a remarkable 13 days.

… and recorded?

Actors receive their scripts a few days before recording, which takes place every four weeks in a state-of-the-art studio at the BBC's premises in the Mailbox complex in central Birmingham. Twenty-four episodes are recorded digitally in six intensive days, using only two hours of studio time per thirteen-minute episode. This schedule means that being an *Archers* actor is by no means a full-time job, even for major characters, so many also have careers in film, theatre, television or other radio drama.

What's that 'dum-di-dum' tune?

The Archers' signature tune is a 'maypole dance': 'Barwick Green', from the suite *My Native Heath* by Yorkshire composer Arthur Wood.

How did you get that news item in?

Episodes are transmitted three to six weeks after recording. But listeners are occasionally intrigued to hear topical events reflected in that evening's broadcast, a feat achieved through a flurry of rewriting, re-recording and editing on the day of transmission.

CHARACTERS BY FORENAME

The characters in this book are listed alphabetically by surname or nickname. If you only know the forename, this should help you locate the relevant entry.

Abbie Tucker
Adam Macy
Alan Franks
Alice Aldridge
Alistair Lloyd
Amy Franks
Annabelle Schrivener
Ben Archer
Bert Fry
Bob Pullen
Brenda Tucker
Brian Aldridge
Bunty and Reg Hebden
Caroline Sterling
Christine Barford
Christopher Carter
Clarrie Grundy
Clive Horrobin
Daniel Hebden Lloyd
David Archer
Debbie Aldridge
Deepak Gupta
Derek and Pat Fletcher
Ed Grundy
Eddie Grundy
Edgar and Eileen Titcombe
Elizabeth Pargetter
Emma Grundy

Fallon Rogers
Freda Fry
George Grundy
Graham Ryder
Hayley Tucker
Hazel Woolley
Heather Pritchard
Helen Archer
Ian Craig
Jack Woolley
Jamie Perks
Jennifer Aldridge
Jill Archer
Jim Lloyd
Joe Grundy
Jolene Perks
Josh Archer
Kate Madikane
Kathy Perks
Kenton Archer
Kirsty Miller
Lewis Carmichael
Lilian Bellamy
Lily and Freddie Pargetter
Lucas Madikane
Lynda Snell
Mabel Thompson
Mandy and India Beesborough
Marshall Latham

Matt Crawford
Maurice Horton
Mike Tucker
Neil Carter
Neville and Nathan Booth
Nic Hanson
Nigel Pargetter
Oliver Sterling
Pat Archer
Peggy Woolley
Phil Archer
Phoebe Aldridge
Pip Archer
Rachel Dorsey
Robert Snell
Roy Tucker
Ruairi Donovan
Ruth Archer
Sabrina and Richard Thwaite
Satya Khanna
Shula Hebden Lloyd
Sid Perks
Stephen Chalkman
Susan Carter
Tom Archer
Tony Archer
Usha Franks
Wayne Foley
William Grundy

Some can also be found under 'Silent Characters'

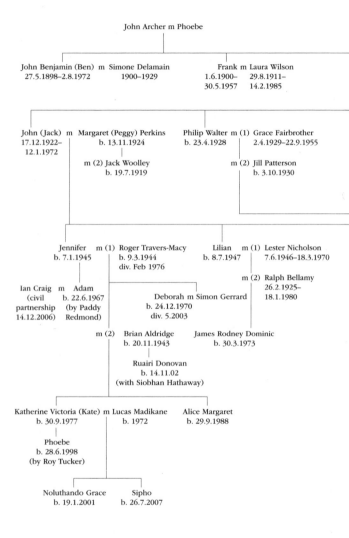

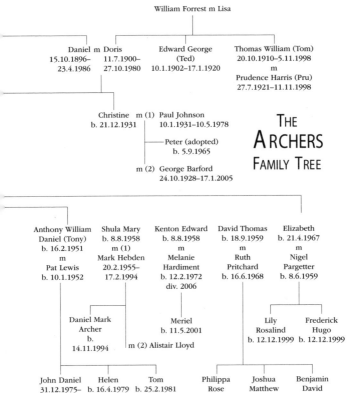

THE ARCHERS FAMILY TREE

William Forrest m Lisa

Daniel m Doris
15.10.1896–
23.4.1986

11.7.1900–
27.10.1980

Edward George
(Ted)
10.1.1902–17.1.1920

Thomas William (Tom)
20.10.1910–5.11.1998
m
Prudence Harris (Pru)
27.7.1921–11.11.1998

Christine   m (1)   Paul Johnson
b. 21.12.1931   10.1.1931–10.5.1978

Peter (adopted)
b. 5.9.1965

m (2)   George Barford
24.10.1928–17.1.2005

Anthony William
Daniel (Tony)
b. 16.2.1951
m
Pat Lewis
b. 10.1.1952

Shula Mary
b. 8.8.1958
m (1)
Mark Hebden
20.2.1955–
17.2.1994

Kenton Edward
b. 8.8.1958
m
Melanie
Hardiment
b. 12.2.1972
div. 2006

David Thomas
b. 18.9.1959
m
Ruth
Pritchard
b. 16.6.1968

Elizabeth
b. 21.4.1967
m
Nigel
Pargetter
b. 8.6.1959

Daniel Mark
Archer
b.
14.11.1994

Meriel
b. 11.5.2001

m (2) Alistair Lloyd

Lily
Rosalind
b. 12.12.1999

Frederick
Hugo
b. 12.12.1999

John Daniel
31.12.1975–
25.2.1998

Helen
b. 16.4.1979

Tom
b. 25.2.1981

Philippa
Rose
(Pip)
b. 17.2.1993

Joshua
Matthew
(Josh)
b. 13.9.1997

Benjamin
David
b. 15.3.2002

ALICE ALDRIDGE

Home Farm/Southampton University • Born 29.9.88
(Hollie Chapman)

Alice is the product of a privileged background – private school, her own horse and a cut-glass accent to match. But this little rich girl had a lot of growing up to do when her father **Brian** brought home her illicit half-brother **Ruairi Donovan**. Alice determined to be as independent as possible, taking a job as a chambermaid at **Grey Gables** (Jennifer was appalled) and applying to join the RAF. A gap year working at an AIDS orphanage in South Africa with elder sister **Kate Madikane** helped put things in perspective and when Alice returned to **Ambridge** she'd managed to shake off her feelings of revulsion for Brian's misdeeds. So much so that when her application for RAF sponsorship of her engineering degree failed, she was able to accept Brian's offer of financial support – but only as a loan. In September 2008, Alice hooked up with **Christopher Carter** – just for a bit of pre-university fun, she said.

BRIAN ALDRIDGE

Home Farm • Born 20.11.43

(Charles Collingwood)

Brian has sailed close to the wind in the past but **Jennifer** always managed to forgive his extra-marital affairs, partly for the comfortable life this wealthy farmer has been able to give her. But when Brian's mistress Siobhan Hathaway bore him **Ruairi Donovan** and then tragically died, leaving him to care for his son, the Aldridge marriage was assailed as never before. Brian's relationship with his other children suffered too, especially as Brian re-drafted his will to make his tiny son a future part-owner of the farm. Jennifer was forced to threaten divorce before Brian gave step-son and daughter **Adam Macy** and **Debbie Aldridge** management control. With a small child to raise, Jennifer was delighted to have a retired husband to share the burden. But uncomfortable Brian found the state a rather unnatural one.

DEBBIE ALDRIDGE

(née Travers-Macy, formerly Gerrard)
Home Farm • Born 24.12.70
(Tamsin Greig)

In some ways Debbie used to be closer to her step-father **Brian Aldridge** than her mother **Jennifer** was. But Debbie is a straight arrow and Brian's affairs – reminding Debbie horribly of her own failed marriage to adulterer Simon Gerrard – severed the ties that once bound them so warmly. Debbie's farm management skills are much in demand. Joint manager of **Home Farm** with brother **Adam Macy**, she also manages the **Estate**'s arable land and a Hungarian dairy farm for a consortium in which Brian has an interest. Happy to keep a safe distance from Brian, she spends most of her time in Hungary, and it was there that she met her boyfriend, fellow farm manager **Marshall Latham**.

JENNIFER ALDRIDGE

(née Archer, formerly Travers-Macy)
Home Farm • Born 7.1.45
(Angela Piper)

Elegant and a great cook, Jennifer loves being a mother and put her early career as a teacher and writer on hold to devote herself to her family. Pregnant by a local farm hand, unmarried Jennifer gave birth to **Adam** (now **Macy**) in 1967. She later married Roger Travers-Macy, who adopted Adam. They had a daughter **Debbie** but the marriage didn't last and Jennifer wed **Brian** in 1976. More daughters followed: **Kate** (now **Madikane**) and **Alice**, who left school when Jennifer was in her sixties. Jennifer thought she had finished her parenting and was looking forward to more grandmotherly times with Kate's daughter **Phoebe**. So you can imagine the torment she endured before agreeing to take Brian's illegitimate child **Ruairi Donovan** into her home. It's a tough woman who could shoulder that commitment. She's **Peggy Woolley**'s daughter, all right.

PHOEBE ALDRIDGE

Willow Farm • Born 28.6.98
(Scarlett Wakelin)

At first sight, you'd naturally assume that **Hayley Tucker** was Phoebe's mother, but the differing surnames tell the real story. Phoebe's real mum is in fact **Kate Madikane**, who in her hippy days had an incongruous relationship with clean-cut **Roy Tucker** and who now lives in Johannesburg. Phoebe was born in a tepee at the Glastonbury Festival and named in a New Age ceremony on Lakey Hill. In Roy and Hayley's care, the bulk of her upbringing has been less colourful, if rather more stable. Phoebe was delighted at the arrival of her new sister **Abbie Tucker**, and they make a lovely, close family, cheerfully coping with the unpredictable occasional visits of exotic 'Mummy Kate'.

AMBRIDGE

Picture a traditional English village. The image in your head is probably not a million miles from Ambridge. Village green with duckpond? Check. Village Hall? Check. Half-timbered pub? Check (**The Bull**). **Village Shop**? Check (thanks to **Jack Woolley**). Ludicrously priced thatched cottages, unsympathetic modern infill and early morning departures by grey-faced commuters? Check, check and check. Gorgeous views and rubbish bus service? Checkity check. But this icon of traditionalism is trying to play its part in the very 21st-century fight against global climate change. Thanks to the leadership of **Pat Archer**, in 2008 Ambridge joined towns such as Totnes and Stroud as one of the UK's 'transition communities'.

AMBRIDGE HALL

'... Are you seeking a short break in the heart of the English countryside? Look no further than our charming guesthouse! All rooms planned by myself, hostess **Lynda Snell***, in accordance with the principles of Feng Shui. Special diets and allergies catered for with understanding and sympathy. I am myself a martyr to hay fever, and have created a low-allergen area of our extensive gardens as an elegant refuge for we sneezers and snufflers! Guests of a literary bent will be intrigued by our Shakespearean plot, using only plants named by the Bard! And visitors of all ages (well-behaved children are of course welcome) cannot fail to be delighted by our trio of llamas in the adjacent paddock...'*

Entry on the **Ambridge** village website.

AMBRIDGE ORGANICS

Not a 'farm shop' exactly, as they are usually on the farm itself, but the 'farm's shop' – **Bridge Farm**'s, that is. Ambridge Organics is owned by **Pat** and **Tony Archer** and managed by their daughter **Helen**, employing **silent** Anja and **Kirsty Miller**, former girlfriend of Helen's brother **Tom**. The shop provides an ethical alternative to **Underwoods**' food hall, selling Bridge Farm veg, yoghurt and ice cream, plus a whole range of bought-in organic produce.

BEN ARCHER

Brookfield Farm • Born 15.3.02

(Thomas Lester)

When **Ruth** became pregnant with Ben it was a double blessing, coming as it did after her recovery from breast cancer. Ruth and **David** have to remind themselves of this when their 'blessed' offspring is fighting with his elder siblings **Josh** and **Pip**, or causing the sort of havoc that energetic small children are prone to do.

DAVID ARCHER

Brookfield Farm • Born 18.9.59

(Timothy Bentinck)

Husband to **Ruth**, devoted father to **Pip**, **Josh** and **Ben**, stalwart of the **Ambridge** cricket team and a parish councillor. Having taken on **Brookfield Farm** in 2001 (much to the disgruntlement of squabbling siblings **Elizabeth Pargetter** and **Kenton**), it seemed like a good idea to recruit specialist herdsman Sam Batton to maximise the revenue from their expanded dairy herd. But in 2006 David's former fiancée Sophie Barlow reappeared, with an adulterous agenda. David spurned her advances too late to stop unhappy Ruth nearly sleeping with Sam. With both third parties off the scene, David worked hard to rebuild his marriage. His support for Ruth over her breast reconstruction, and working together on projects such as the proposed Ambridge Heat and Power green energy plant, helped re-bond this naturally secure couple.

HELEN ARCHER

Bridge Farm • Born 16.4.79

(Louiza Patikas)

For a while, two bereavements caused **Pat** and **Tony Archer**'s daughter significant psychological problems. Her elder brother John died in an accident in 1998 and her partner Greg Turner committed suicide in 2004. Driven Helen's attempts to control her unhappy life led to anorexia and, in 2006, to uncontrolled drinking and partying. Time at a specialist clinic helped her recover from the former. Counselling – plus the shock of injuring **Mike Tucker** while drink-driving – helped her understand and control the latter. With greater equilibrium, she returned to her busy life, drawing on her HND in food technology to manufacture **Borsetshire** Blue cheese and managing the farm's shop **Ambridge Organics**.

JILL ARCHER

(née Patterson)
Glebe Cottage • Born 3.10.30
(Patricia Greene)

To the despair of feminists, Jill Archer would probably describe herself as a mother and retired farmer's wife. It may be defining her by the others in her life, but it is an entirely accurate label. In 2007 she and **Phil** celebrated their ruby wedding anniversary, along the way raising **Kenton, Shula** (now **Hebden Lloyd**), **David** and **Elizabeth** (now **Pargetter**). Jill has been actively involved in village life and on the farm – in fact she still tends **Brookfield**'s bees and hens – and many villagers have benefited from her motherly instincts. But Jill herself would be the first to point out that 'caring' doesn't mean 'doormat'. She'll fight her corner fiercely on important family matters or wider issues such as hunting. She's a committed 'anti', as **Oliver Sterling** knows to his cost.

JOSH ARCHER

Brookfield Farm • Born 13.9.97

(George Bingham)

Like many small boys (and big boys too, come to that), **David** and **Ruth**'s middle child has occasional wild enthusiasms. Previously attached to a charming plaything called a Killer Borg, in 2006 Josh took pity on an abandoned muntjac deer. Against their better judgement, his parents succumbed to Josh's piteous pestering and for a while the lad did keep his promise to look after 'Monty', even sharing his bed with him, to **Bert Fry**'s considerable disapproval. But eventually the novelty faded, so the beast was found a new home at **Lower Loxley Hall**. Monty, that is; not Josh.

KENTON ARCHER

April Cottage • Born 8.8.58
(Richard Attlee)

Kenton sees himself as a bon viveur and wit. Others would say he's more bonkers and a twit. But in recent years he's managed to defy his previous failures in business (having been bailed out by parents **Phil** and **Jill** at least twice) and has successfully held down a job as manager of **Jaxx Caff**. In 2007 he moved in with girlfriend **Kathy Perks**, supporting her superbly when she bravely gave evidence in a traumatic rape trial the following year. Kenton makes a wonderful 'uncle' to Kathy's son **Jamie**. In fact, being an uncle is probably what he does best and he's very popular with the Archer children, if not always with their parents. Kenton has a daughter, Meriel, who lives in New Zealand. According to his ex-wife Mel, this is only just far enough away.

PAT ARCHER

(née Lewis)
Bridge Farm • Born 10.1.52
(Patricia Gallimore)

Pat's been fighting for the environment most of her adult life. She and **Tony** converted **Bridge Farm** to organic as early as 1984 and Pat developed a thriving business processing their milk into yoghurt and ice cream. Although plodding Tony knows he's benefited from Pat's militant enthusiasm, there are times when he wishes for a quieter life. In 2008, Pat caused ructions by opposing close family members' plans for an anaerobic digester at **Home Farm**. Idealistic daughter **Helen** supported Pat, who felt that the land should be used for growing food for local consumption, rather than energy crops, while her more pragmatic son **Tom** sided with his father. Tony rightly predicted that the campaign would cause bad feeling for little effect. Pat consoled herself by leading an initiative to turn **Ambridge** into a sustainable 'transition community'.

PHIL ARCHER

Glebe Cottage • Born 23.4.28

(Norman Painting)

The 23rd of April is associated with three icons of England: Shakespeare, St George and Phil Archer. Through the 1960s and 1970s, Phil built up **Brookfield Farm**, finally passing it to son **David** and daughter-in-law **Ruth** in 2001. He's a staunch churchgoer – in fact, he's the church organist – and his marriage to **Jill** has been one of the most stable relationships in **Ambridge**. In his retirement, Phil is very active, looking after Brookfield's previously neglected garden as well as his own; and his piano playing is always in demand for village productions. Phil sometimes overestimates the musical talents of his granddaughter **Pip**, but in all other respects most reckon him to be an admirable man – although he's more likely to be found star-gazing than writing plays or slaying dragons.

PIP ARCHER

Brookfield Farm • Born 17.2.93
(Helen Monks)

Like many teenagers, Pip has multiple personalities. At times she's a delight, particularly when she's taking an interest in the cows. But she's also reached the age that parents wish could be fast-forwarded, when the simplest request can be met with stentorian huffing and vertebrae-threatening head tossing. In 2007, Pip joined Young Farmers and enthusiastically threw herself into activities from disco dancing to cattle judging. She also found a boyfriend, Jonathan, and this step to independence inevitably raised more chances for friction with her parents **Ruth** and **David**. As can often be the case at this tricky time, Pip sometimes gets on better with grandfather **Phil**, especially as she has inherited some of his musical talent. As well as playing the piano and clarinet, Pip sings in the choir at **Borchester** Green school with her friend **Izzy**.

RUTH ARCHER

(née Pritchard)
Brookfield Farm • Born 16.6.68
(Felicity Finch)

In 2008 Ruth had a breast reconstruction, following a mastectomy because of cancer eight years earlier. It was the culmination of a tumultuous period, which could have seen Ruth's marriage to **David** blown apart by her – fortunately unconsummated – affair with the **Brookfield** herdsman Sam Batton. After Sam's departure, Ruth returned to her former role managing and milking Brookfield's dairy herd, while sharing with David the care of their children **Pip**, **Josh** and **Ben**. We can be sure that Ruth could have predicted very little of this in 1987 when she arrived at Brookfield as a fresh-faced agricultural student from Prudhoe in Northumberland.

TOM ARCHER

1, The Green • Born 25.2.81

(Tom Graham)

Ambitious Tom has had a few setbacks in his journey to become the sausage king of **Borsetshire**. It was only the intervention in 2005 of his hard-nosed uncle **Brian Aldridge** which saved Tom's over-extended organic pork business, and the uneasy relationship has caused friction with Tom's more idealistic parents **Pat** and **Tony**. But at least things went from strength to strength with Tom's girlfriend **Brenda Tucker** (sister of his friend **Roy**) and they moved in together in 2007. As Tom regained his confidence he set up a mobile catering company, Tom Archer's Gourmet Grills, and in 2008 outfaced Brian enough to rejoin the organic movement with a small herd back at **Bridge Farm**.

TONY ARCHER

Bridge Farm • Born 16.2.51
(Colin Skipp)

Tony faces the unrelenting daily round of milking and the punishing demands of year-round veg production with a resigned weariness. The signs of age? No, he's been like that most of his adult life. He keeps plugging away, committed – like wife **Pat** – to the organic cause and trying not to think of the plush lives of his sisters **Jennifer Aldridge** and **Lilian Bellamy**. In 2008, after one run-in too many with rapacious landlords **Borchester Land**, Tony took a big step to becoming a property owner, when he and Pat made moves to buy the freehold of **Bridge Farm**. Tony probably celebrated with a pint or three of Shires, and maybe a spin in his classic MG Midget. But not at the same time. That's what got daughter **Helen** into so much trouble.

BAGGY

Borchester

Baggy, Snatch Foster and **Eddie Grundy** were once the Freeman, Hardy and Willis of **Borsetshire**; they always had something afoot. Although (unlike those celebrated shoe-sellers) it was usually something dodgy. But Snatch took it a dodge too far with his illegal meat scam, so Baggy is now Eddie's main accomplice, often helping with the spectrum of Grundy activities, from laying patios to poaching – and we don't mean eggs.

CHRISTINE BARFORD

(née Archer, formerly Johnson)
Woodbine Cottage • Born 21.12.31
(Lesley Saweard)

Phil **Archer**'s younger sister Chris – as she's always known in the family – lives a quiet retirement after many years running a riding stable (now owned by her niece **Shula Hebden Lloyd**) and two very different marriages. Peter, her adopted son from her first marriage, travels a lot as an administrator with a symphony orchestra. After the death of Peter's flaky father Paul Johnson, Chris found more secure happiness with solid, dependable George Barford. But sadly George died in 2005 while they were waiting to re-occupy their house after a horrific firebomb attack. Arsonist **Clive Horrobin** was targeting his long-time enemy: gamekeeper and former policeman George. He was sentenced to 12 years but it wasn't much comfort to Chris, who had to face life as a widow for the second time. In 2008, she became a churchwarden at **St Stephen's**.

MANDY AND INDIA BEESBOROUGH

Mandy born 1953, India born 1988
Loxley Barratt

The red-haired, vivacious doyenne of the Pony Club has produced a similarly luscious and horsey daughter. India Beesborough is a friend and former schoolmate of **Alice Aldridge**. **Susan Carter** nurses the hope that her son **Christopher** might hook up with India one day. **Jennifer Aldridge** nurses the hope that her husband **Brian** doesn't hook up (again, it's rumoured) with Mandy.

LILIAN BELLAMY

(née Archer, formerly Nicholson)
The Dower House • Born 8.7.47
(Sunny Ormonde)

After many louche years as a tax exile in Guernsey following the death of her second husband Ralph, Lilian returned to **Ambridge** apparently with the intention of teaching her siblings **Jennifer Aldridge** and **Tony Archer** the true meaning of the word 'embarrassment'. Lilian has certainly ignored the adage 'never go back'. In 2006 she bought a majority share in **The Bull**, the pub in which she'd grown up, and moved back into the home she'd once shared with Ralph. This time it was with her 'Tiger' **Matt Crawford**, who seems to delight in pushing the boundaries of the relationship. Most people think they deserve each other. Lilian's son James (born in 1973) paid her a rare visit in 2005 but sadly his only objective was getting a shedload of money to shore up an over-ambitious property deal.

NEVILLE AND NATHAN BOOTH

Neville born 1949
Ambridge

Bell-ringer Neville Booth has attracted a surprising amount of unwarranted controversy over the years. When **Jolene Perks** (then Rogers) took advantage of **Kathy**'s absence to have a night of illicit passion with **Sid**, she parked her car away from **The Bull**. Unfortunately word got around that she'd appeared to spend the night at Mr Booth's house! And more recently **Bert Fry** described Neville as a 'Casanova in casual shoes' in the mistaken belief that he was making a play for **Freda**. Neville's nephew Nathan has a rather more deserved reputation for unpleasantness. Someone should have told him that when you've been caught cheating in a nettle-eating contest (he numbed his mouth with ice cubes), your chances of election to the parish council are slim. 'Slimy' is the word most often used to describe him.

BORCHESTER

Although **Felpersham** provides most of what passes for the bright lights in **Borsetshire**, this market town also has much to offer. Six miles north-east of **Ambridge**, Borchester still retains a historic core, with its clock tower and wool market. Shops include **Underwoods** department store and **Ambridge Organics**. Mental recreation is catered for by the Theatre Royal and multiplex cinema (well, all right, three screens) and more physical pursuits by the gym and swimming pool at the municipal leisure centre. And then you can throw all that good work away in many cafés and restaurants, including **Jaxx Caff** and the upmarket Botticelli's – or completely down the tubes at pubs such as the comfortable George, the Tin of Peaches (near the canning factory) and the lively Goat and Nightgown, near the General Hospital and Borchester College.

BORCHESTER LAND

This property company has upset more than a few **Ambridge** residents in its aggressive pursuit of return on capital. BL owns the Berrow **Estate**, whose 1,020 arable acres are managed by **Debbie Aldridge**. In August 2008, former part-timer Pete was appointed temporary gamekeeper at the pheasant shoot, when **Will Grundy** took leave of absence. There is a small set of business units at Sawyer's Farm and in 2003 BL converted a few acres of agricultural land for the luxury housing development **Grange Spinney**. The company is chaired by **Matt Crawford**, who on the hard-nosed scale comes somewhere between titanium and granite. His board members include **Brian Aldridge**, **Annabelle Schrivener** and long-term Crawford crony **Stephen** 'Chalky' **Chalkman**. Former tenants **Pat** and **Tony Archer** at **Bridge Farm** were delighted when they started to slip their landlord's clutches in 2008.

BORSETSHIRE

Borsetshire is not exactly a real land re-labelled, like Hardy's Wessex, but it has a lot in common with the counties of Warwickshire and Worcestershire to the south and south-west of Birmingham. This attractive rural area is dominated to the east by the cathedral city and administrative centre of **Felpersham**. The second largest settlement is the market town of **Borchester**. **Ambridge** lies south-east of the Hassett Hills and falls under South Borsetshire District Council. The main local newspapers are the *Felpersham Advertiser* and the *Borchester Echo*, although the upstart *Westbury Courier* is making a name for itself with stunts and promotions. The area also has its own radio station named, with impressive clarity, Radio Borsetshire.

BRIDGE FARM

STOCK

92 milkers (Friesians) • 45 followers (heifers/calves)
45 fattening pigs

CROPS

115 acres grassland • 15 acres barley • 20 acres wheat
5 acres potatoes • 4 acres carrots • 2 acres leeks
3 acres swedes • 2 acres Dutch cabbage
1 acre Savoy cabbage
5 acres mixed vegetable and salad crops,
including two polytunnels

LABOUR

Tony Archer • **Pat Archer** • **Tom Archer**
Helen Archer • **Jazzer** (part-time, pigs)
Clarrie Grundy (dairy) • Colin Kennedy (dairy)

Tony and **Pat Archer** rent 140 acres from the **Estate**, with an extra 32 acres from other landlords. Bridge Farm converted to organic in 1984. The farm's produce – including cheese, yoghurt and ice cream made in their own dairy – is sold through a wholesaler and to local outlets including **Ambridge Organics**. In 2008, **Tom** re-established a small herd of organic pigs, and Pat and Tony made moves to buy their freehold.

BROOKFIELD FARM

STOCK

180 milkers (Friesians) • 79 followers (heifers/calves –
some Brown Swiss cross) • 85 beef cattle (Herefords)
325 ewes • Hens (small scale)

CROPS

339 acres grassland • 88 acres cereals • 10 acres
oilseed rape • 10 acres potatoes • 12 acres beans
10 acres forage maize

LABOUR

David Archer (managing)
Ruth Archer (managing and herdsperson)
Eddie Grundy (relief herdsperson)
Bert Fry (retired, casual) • Biff (sheepdog)

Brookfield is a 469-acre mixed farm incorporating the old holdings of Marney's and Hollowtree. After **Phil**'s retirement in 2001, **David** and **Ruth** contracted out the arable work to **Home Farm** and expanded the dairy herd. Brookfield is doing its best to move away from selling its products as commodities and to get closer to the customer. High-quality beef from the Herefords is sold online and at the farm gate, and the lamb is marketed co-operatively under the Hassett Hills brand.

THE BULL

George Orwell once described a mythical perfect pub: The Moon Under Water. We think he'd like a lot of **Ambridge**'s only remaining local. A half-timbered building near the village green, The Bull offers excellent Shires ales, genial bar service from **Sid** and **Jolene Perks**, and **Freda Fry**'s home-cooked food. It still retains the traditional two bars, one being called the Ploughman's, and has a range of satisfyingly physical activities including darts, skittles and boules. There's even a pet peacock, Eccles, in the beer garden. However, Mr Orwell might be bemused by the small cyber area with two internet-linked computers. He'd certainly blanch at the music nights which **Fallon Rogers** organises in the upstairs function room. And we're sure he'd think the big screen, deployed for major sporting events, was far too redolent of Big Brother.

LEWIS CARMICHAEL

Lower Loxley Hall
(Robert Lister)

Everyone agreed that Lewis, suave and likable as he is, deserved more than a mere six months with **Nigel Pargetter**'s mother Julia, but sadly her death in November 2005 brought their happy marriage (the second for each of them) to a sudden end. Although retired, architect Lewis still does the occasional job that interests him, most recently the deceptively tricky extension and division of the house at **Willow Farm** into two dwellings. It leaves him plenty of time to lend a hand at **Lower Loxley**, running the art gallery or even (brave man) looking after the Pargetter twins **Lily and Freddie**.

CHRISTOPHER CARTER

Ambridge View • Born 22.6.88

(William Sanderson-Thwaite)

Like his father **Neil**, Chris is a keen cricketer and a bell-ringer. He sounded the death knell for **Susan**'s hopes that at least one Carter would gain a degree when he announced in 2004 that he wanted to pursue a career as a farrier. But Neil was delighted when **Ronnie** took his son on. Chris successfully completed the four-year training scheme and his developing musculature made him a popular visitor to the area's stables and riding schools. And once Chris had letters after his name, Susan realised how proud she was of him. She also relished her son's close proximity to the horse-owning classes. Even though he dumped the Lord Lieutenant's niece Venetia Streatfield to go out with a part-time barmaid from the wrong end of **Borchester**, in the summer of 2008 he took up with another 'posh totty': **Alice Aldridge**.

NEIL CARTER

Ambridge View • Born 22.5.57
(Brian Hewlett)

Neil lives 'above the shop', which for him is a house he built himself on eight acres near **Willow Farm**. This (the land, not the house) contains his herd of organic Gloucester Old Spot pigs, and the free-range hens which he runs with **Hayley Tucker**. Normally easy-going (some would say staid), bell-ringer Neil is tower captain at **St Stephen's** and in 2008 he became a churchwarden. In the past, his attitude to **Ed Grundy** was far from Christian (some would say with good reason). He was very unhappy when daughter **Emma** (also **Grundy**) got back together with Ed, but gradually realised that Ed had matured.

SUSAN CARTER

(née Horrobin)
Ambridge View • Born 10.10.63
(Charlotte Martin)

The high-fliers among us might think that managing the **Village Shop** and post office isn't much to write home about. But when that home was originally 6, The Green – the chaotic headquarters of the infamous **Horrobin** family – it's actually quite a step up. Susan's climb to respectability has been a rocky one. She even went to prison in 1993 when forced to shelter her fugitive criminal brother **Clive**. Susan has had to accept that husband **Neil** will always be a pigman, and is realising that son **Christopher** should have a good career ahead of him as a farrier. But when daughter **Emma Grundy** moved back in with ex brother-in-law **Ed Grundy**, Susan was mortified. As the centre of the village bush telegraph she prefers to talk disapprovingly of others, not be on the receiving end herself.

CASA NUEVA

The gamekeeper's tied cottage at **Home Farm** is in quite an isolated spot, on a lane bordering Lyttleton Covert. **Will** and **Emma Grundy** returned from their Mexican honeymoon and named their home 'new house' in Spanish, hoping to lay to rest the ghost of the previous resident, Will's boss Greg Turner, who had committed suicide nearby. Sadly, the Curse of Greg could not be exorcised so easily, and the marriage was soon over. And Will's second attempt at cosy domesticity, with **Nic Hanson**, was equally ill-starred. Despite these setbacks, Will remained, trying to make the place as cosy a second home for his son **George** as it could be, until the pain of **Ed** and Emma reuniting became too much and Will had to move away for a while.

STEPHEN CHALKMAN

Borchester

(Stephen Critchlow)

Stephen Chalkman is the Hare to **Matt Crawford**'s Burke, the two of them unearthing dubious money-making opportunities all over the county. 'Chalky' is a former member of South **Borsetshire** District Council's planning committee; 'former' because he once neglected to mention his wife's involvement in a planning application which the committee was considering. The application subsequently became **Grange Spinney** and Chalkman became a director of **Borchester Land**. When Matt was trying to hide money during his divorce, he 'paid' Chalkman a large sum as Matt's 'financial consultant'. Matt also 'lost' £50,000 to his old mate in a well-staged poker game, complete with upstanding landowner **Nigel Pargetter** as a witness. In 2005, the partners in, er… business invested in the conversion of the old Cat and Fiddle pub to luxury flats, scuppering **Lynda Snell**'s hopes of turning it into a heritage centre.

IAN CRAIG

Honeysuckle Cottage • Born 1970
(Stephen Kennedy)

G rey Gables' head chef 'married' **Adam Macy** in a civil partnership in 2006. **Sid Perks** is still uncomfortable having a gay couple living just across the green, as are a few other villagers, but most find this affable Northern Irelander good company. He certainly gets on well with Adam's little 'nephew' **Ruairi Donovan**, although Ruairi's father **Brian Aldridge** has never totally put to rest the fears of the 'mixed messages' which he feels might confuse Ruairi's development. Ian would like a child of his own, and was badly used by Madeleine (Madds), an old friend who dangled the possibility only to snatch it away when she found a permanent partner. It severely tested Ian's relationship with Adam but the two came though stronger in the end – especially when Ian proposed, knowing that he'd have to come out to his traditional Ulster farming family.

MATT CRAWFORD

The Dower House • Born 7.8.47
(Kim Durham)

In 2008, Matt's partner **Lilian Bellamy** discovered to her surprise that Matt had been adopted. She persuaded Matt to meet his birth mother, but the reunion was unsuccessful. An amateur psychologist (aren't we all – except for you professional psychologists, anyway) might conclude that Matt's early feelings of alienation lay behind his ruthless rise from the backstreets of London to conspicuous business success. Chairman of **Borchester Land** and a property speculator in his own right, Matt frequently sails close to the wind to get what he wants. And not just in business, either. Coming out of an expensive divorce with Yvette, Matt bought Ambridge's finest residence – The Dower House – as a suitable home for him and Lilian. But soon this inveterate gambler was risking the relationship by dallying with other women, including briefly the redoubtable **Annabelle Schrivener**.

RUAIRI DONOVAN

Home Farm • Born 14.11.02
(Matthew Rocket)

Ruairi is – in a word that 21st-century mores have made rather archaic – the illegitimate product of an extra-marital affair between **Brian Aldridge** and the deceased Siobhan Hathaway (née Donovan). When Brian made the choice to stay with **Jennifer** rather than starting a new life with Siobhan, he imagined that his relationship with Ruairi (pronounced 'Rory') would be tenuous at best, especially when Siobhan moved to Germany. But her death from cancer in May 2007 brought the child – after mighty ructions – to **Home Farm**. Jennifer made heroic, nay saintly, efforts and even Brian applied himself to hands-on fatherhood in a way his older children had missed out on. Whether their work will compensate for the loss of Ruairi's real mother and his transplantation to a wealthy but fragile environment are yet to be seen.

RACHEL DORSEY

Felpersham

(Deborah McAndrew)

Rachel arrived as archdeacon of **Felpersham** diocese in 2007. Rachel and **Ambridge**'s vicar **Alan Franks** have a similar, modernising outlook and she soon encouraged him to embark on radical projects such as the proposal to remove the pews from **St Stephen's** – eventually narrowly rejected by the PCC. To the consternation of some of the more traditional parishioners, Rachel was very supportive of Alan's engagement to **Usha** (then Gupta) and in fact presided over one of their marriage services – the Christian one, naturally – in August 2008.

THE ESTATE

More correctly, the Berrow Estate: see **Borchester Land**.

FAT PAUL

There are quite a few Fat Pauls around. One is a DJ, another a guitarist in a punk band. Our Fat Paul – building contractor Paul Blocker – has musically related talents too. Sort of. He managed to squeeze himself into the cab of his JCB to perform a comically awful 'Disco Diggers' routine with friend **Eddie Grundy** at the 2001 **Ambridge** fête. But even more memorable than that is his party piece. If you should ever hear the sounds of Black Lace's pineapple-pushing mega-hit 'Agadoo', you'd be well advised to run, and not just to retain your musical credibility. Paul's Pavlovian response to this musical masterpiece is to start shedding his size XXXL clothes. Don't say we didn't warn you.

FELPERSHAM

Birmingham lies some 30 miles from **Ambridge**, many of whose more recent arrivals commute there every day. But for most purposes the cathedral city of Felpersham fits the bill. Only 17 miles to the east of the village, the county town of **Borsetshire** is well stocked with shops, eating places and opportunities for night-time excess.

DEREK AND PAT FLETCHER

Glebelands

For many years, **Ambridge** parish council was under the popular chairmanship first of **Jack Woolley** and then of **Christine Barford**'s husband George. Then on George's death came... Derek Fletcher. More 'little England' than 'middle England', Derek and Pat occupy a gnome-encircled 'executive home' in Glebelands – the **Grange Spinney** of its day. Along with **Peggy Woolley**, Derek was one of the parishioners unable to accept a woman vicar at **St Stephen's** and has been known to send anonymous poison pen letters, too. He is still trying to get over the arrival in the village of **Usha Franks** (née Gupta) – and that happened in 1991. Her marriage to the Reverend **Alan** just confirmed Derek's belief that the country was going to the dogs.

WAYNE FOLEY

Borchester

(Ian Brooker)

'... If you think your life's insane
You should listen in to Wayne
He's the maddest one round here
He loves Radio Borsetshire...'

Trail for Wayne Foley's afternoon show on Radio Borsetshire,
87.3FM

ALAN FRANKS

The Vicarage, Ambridge
(John Telfer)

On 29 August 2008, Alan Franks married **Usha** (née Gupta). Nothing remarkable in that, you might think; mixed marriages are not unusual nowadays. But when you learn that Alan is the vicar of **Ambridge**, Penny Hassett, Darrington and Edgeley, and Usha is a practising Hindu, you'll understand that he isn't a man to fear controversy. Formerly an accountant, Alan worked as a non-stipendary minister in Nottingham before taking the cloth full-time after the death in 1995 of his first wife Catherine (who was black). He's attempted some radical innovations, although his plan to remove the pews at **St Stephen's** was a step too far for the PCC. Alan's Christian faith is bolstered by a strong sense of social justice, and he has fathered a similar firebrand in his daughter **Amy**.

AMY FRANKS

The Vicarage/Manchester University • Born 1989
(Vinette Robinson)

There are feisty genes on both sides of Amy's family. Her father **Alan** isn't afraid of a fight and nor is her grandmother **Mabel Thompson** (Amy's mother is dead). This led to fiery times in 2008, as Amy clashed with Mabel, who strongly opposed Alan's marriage to **Usha**. In 2007, Amy started a midwifery degree at Manchester University, distancing her from her one-time best friend in **Ambridge**, **Alice Aldridge**. To be honest, the friendship had already been severely strained by Alice's attempt to join the RAF, a move significantly at odds with Amy's radical views.

USHA FRANKS

(née Gupta)
The Vicarage, Ambridge • Born 17.6.62
(Souad Faress)

Usha married **Alan Franks** on 29 August 2008. Most were happy for them but, as Usha is a practising Hindu and Alan the local vicar, joy was not totally unconfined. **Shula Hebden Lloyd** resigned as churchwarden after her unguarded comments made the local paper (although there's history there: Shula once had an affair with a former boyfriend of Usha's). Usha's patrician father **Deepak** and depressive mother **Sanchali** in Wolverhampton struggled to accept the match and Usha received angry threats from within her own community. This brought back horrible memories of the racist attacks she'd suffered when she first moved to **Ambridge** in 1991. In contrast to Alan's modest stipend, Usha brings big earning power to the marriage, as a partner in Felpersham solicitors Jefferson Crabtree. She relaxes through salsa dancing (with **Ruth Archer**) and playing poker (with anyone foolish enough to underrate her).

BERT FRY

Brookfield Bungalow • Born 1936

(Eric Allan)

There came a man from out the West
Some farming for to try
He worked the land for many years
That man was stout Bert Fry.

Retired from **Brookfield** late in life
He still worked casually
But, gilet wearing, also guided
Guests at **Lower Loxley**.

A champion vintage ploughman
And, like John Clare long before,
Bert is a Ploughman Poet
(And to some a champion bore)

Churchgoing, cricket umpiring
No greater love has he
Than wife of over fifty years
His much-beloved **Fre-**

(-da)

FREDA FRY

Brookfield Bungalow

In 2008, deciding that his wife was becoming rather too fond of the filling meals she served up at home and at **The Bull**, Bert suggested that Freda might like to join **Ambridge**'s new slimming club. He soon learned to 'be careful what you wish for'. His newly svelte spouse underwent a minor makeover and attracted the attentions of **Neville Booth** – at least in jealous Bert's tortured imagination. In fact, Freda's efforts were entirely for the benefit of the man she had loved for over fifty years: Bert himself. Although Freda works in a pub (as well as cleaning the posh holiday home Arkwright Hall) Bert is careful that she doesn't drink there – at least no alcohol. We still don't know what happened, but as Bert will gnomically inform you, they can never go back to Filey…

GRANGE FARM

STOCK
36 milkers (Guernseys)

CROPS
50 acres grassland

LABOUR
Oliver Sterling (managing and relief)
Ed Grundy (herd manager)
Mike Tucker (dairy processing)

A working farm – although some may dispute that description – until the bankrupt **Grundys** were evicted in 2000. The bulk of the acreage was absorbed back into the **Estate** and the farmhouse sold with 50 acres to **Oliver Sterling,** who in 2006 established a small herd of Guernseys to supply **Mike Tucker**'s milk round. With former resident **Ed Grundy** as herd manager, it thrived – until an outbreak of bovine TB in 2008 rocked milk and cheese sales. The normally resilient Oliver would have jacked it all in, but for Ed's determination to weather the storm.

GRANGE SPINNEY

After much controversy, this development of 12 luxury houses and six 'low cost' homes was built by **Borchester Land** in 2003 on a few acres of former farmland. Many of the residents commute to Birmingham and elsewhere and don't play much part in the community. Notable exceptions are **Richard and Sabrina Thwaite**, who have thrown themselves into village life – even if Sabrina's fierce competitiveness has put a few **Ambridge** noses out of joint.

GREY GABLES

'...yes Jack, Grey Gables Hotel. No, you don't own it any more, you sold it to **Caroline** *and* **Oliver Sterling***. Yes, Caroline used to be your manager there. Ooh, years and years. Now this is* **Roy Tucker***. You remember Roy, he's deputy manager. Jean-Paul? No, he left years ago. The head chef's* **Ian Craig** *– the Irishman? Well, never mind. Come on, we're going to have a little swim at the health club. Golf? Maybe we could play a few holes tomorrow. No, you sold the club as well – to* **Borchester Land***? Now this is – oh you know. Yes,* **Lynda Snell** *the receptionist. Sorry Lynda, senior receptionist. Yes Jack, she's very memorable, I agree...'*

Peggy Woolley overheard talking to her husband **Jack.**

CLARRIE GRUNDY

Keeper's Cottage • Born 12.5.54
(Rosalind Adams)

Behind every good man there's a good woman, goes the old saying. To **Eddie**'s credit, he once said that Clarrie wasn't behind him; she'd always been beside him. And she is a very good woman, even if her husband rarely fits that description. Clarrie works incessantly. Not only does she cook and clean for Eddie and curmudgeonly father-in-law **Joe**, she also holds down two jobs, in the dairy at **Bridge Farm** and behind the bar at **The Bull**. On top of this, she is constantly trying to reconcile her two feuding sons **Ed** and **William**. To escape her daily drudgery, Clarrie likes a nice romantic novel (not that she gets much time to read) and very occasionally escapes to Great Yarmouth to see her sister Rosie Mabbott. But her best-ever holidays have been very occasional trips to her beloved France. And in 2008, Will treated her and Eddie to a holiday in Torremolinos, the scene of their honeymoon 27 years earlier.

ED GRUNDY

Rickyard Cottage, Brookfield • Born 28.9.84

(Barry Farrimond)

Few would have backed Ed to become a model employee, as herd manager at **Grange Farm**. He's served community punishments for joyriding and burglary and once tried to grow cannabis in a barn at **Bridge Farm** with his mate **Jazzer**. He's had a complicated relationship with **Emma Grundy** – no, actually she's his former sister-in-law (we said it was complicated). He and Emma tried to make a go of it in 2005 but the strain of living in a caravan with baby **George** became too great and Emma moved back with her parents. Despite his resentment, and the attentions of the admirable **Fallon Rogers**, Ed couldn't bury his love for Emma, and they got back together in 2008. Brother **Will** was furious, Emma's parents dismayed and the rest of the village intrigued to see how things would work out this time.

EDDIE GRUNDY

Keeper's Cottage • Born 15.3.51

(Trevor Harrison)

Eddie works in all shades of the economy, from legitimate casual work on the farms of **Ambridge** – often using his ancient tractor or digger – to a variety of other enterprises, some not even guessed at by the taxman. He's your man for garden ornaments, compost, landscaping, dodgy meat… OK, he admits that last one was a bit of a mistake. With his father **Joe**, Eddie was the tenant of **Grange Farm** before they went bust in 2000. He long ago shelved his hopes of making it big as a country and western singer and now contents himself with being master of **Grundys' Field**.

EMMA GRUNDY

(née Carter)
Rickyard Cottage, Brookfield • Born 7.8.84
(Felicity Jones)

'*I thought my brother-in-law was the father of my child!*' Not the headline in one of those magazines you see at the supermarket checkout, but the real dilemma that once faced Emma over her son **George**. Hardly surprisingly, her marriage to **Will** didn't last long, and nor did a difficult time with that very brother-in-law **Ed**. Back home with her parents **Neil** and **Susan Carter**, Emma tried to buckle down to work – assistant manager of **Jaxx Caff**, cleaning at Honeysuckle Cottage and **Brookfield** – while gradually rebuilding a civilised relationship with her former husband. Will even started to entertain thoughts of them getting back together. But Emma had never stopped loving Ed, and it was with him that she resumed a relationship, in the summer of 2008.

GEORGE GRUNDY

Rickyard Cottage, Brookfield/Casa Nueva
Born 7.4.05

This little chap fitted more familial complications into his first year than many people have in their whole lives. He was named George after **William Grundy**'s former gamekeeping mentor George Barford and Edward after... well, who? Grandfather **Eddie**? Or Will's brother **Ed**, whom **Emma** mistakenly believed to be George's real father? A DNA test proved otherwise. Not much later Emma was divorced from Will and estranged for several years from Ed. Although resident with his mum, George spends regular time with Will, which caused friction for a while when Will's one-time girlfriend **Nic Hanson** was living at **Casa Nueva** with her two children. When Ed and Emma got back together, Will was so distraught that he had to leave the village, even though it meant seeing much less of his beloved son.

JOE GRUNDY

Keeper's Cottage • Born 18.9.21

(Edward Kelsey)

Did you catch that tantalising whiff of liniment and home-made cider, with subtle top notes of horse manure and pipe tobacco? Joe Grundy's probably just passed by. Joe was forced into retirement when he lost **Grange Farm** through bankruptcy, although many say that it was his aversion to effort which lost him the tenancy in the first place. Joe now lets his son do the work (no change there, says **Eddie**) and potters around in the garden at Keeper's Cottage and for **Kathy Perks** at April Cottage next door. The horse manure? That'll be from Joe's pony Bartleby, who pulls the trap which is Joe's main means of transport. In 2008, Joe enjoyed a brief flowering of friendship with Muriel Sommerskill, a visiting former resident. Sadly, this was short-lived. Muriel had to admit to Joe that she was dying of cancer.

WILLIAM GRUNDY

Gloucestershire • Born 9.2.83

(Philip Molloy)

If you're the sort of person who likes taking risks, try telling Will Grundy to count his blessings. On the face of it, Will has done well for himself. He has a lovely, healthy son, **George**, and a responsible job as a gamekeeper. So not only does he have a tied cottage but in 2008 an inheritance enabled him to buy 1, The Green and rent it out. However, these material benefits don't make up for Will's devastated private life. His marriage to George's mother was blown apart, thanks to **Emma**'s longing for Will's brother **Ed**, and his attempts at a new relationship with **Nic Hanson** were knocked for six when he caught Nic smacking George. When Ed and Emma reunited in 2008, tormented Will was forced to swap his job as head keeper at the combined **Grey Gables**, Berrow **Estate** and **Home Farm** shoot for another post in Gloucestershire.

GRUNDYS' FIELD

When **Lynda Snell** is showing her B&B guests round **Ambridge**, she's careful to avoid Grundys' Field. The scrappy pole barn, rough shed and old shipping container aren't the most picturesque sights, admittedly. **Eddie Grundy**'s decrepit tractor and digger don't help. And the gently stewing mounds of compost are hardly a tourist attraction either. But this 3.4 acres is the engine room of Eddie's business activities (very occasionally abetted by **Joe**). They don't just store their garden ornaments and materials for the landscaping business there. In the colder months they raise Christmas turkeys and over-winter sheep for hill farmers. Spring and summer see car-boot sales, with children entertained by the Berkshire sow Barbarella. And year round you should be able to get a pint of home-made cider, as long as you've a strong constitution and a disregard for the excise laws.

DR DEEPAK GUPTA

Tettenhall, Wolverhampton

(Madhav Sharma)

This doctor of medicine (now retired) was a Ugandan Asian who was forced by Idi Amin's expulsion in 1972 to move his family to Britain. Disapproving of his daughter **Usha**'s settling in **Ambridge**, he and his depressive wife kept their distance for many years, letting his sister-in-law **Satya Khanna** and son Shiv be Usha's link to the family. But this changed in 2008 when Usha received threats following her engagement to **Alan Franks**. Perhaps engineered by cunning Satya, Dr Gupta turned up in Ambridge unannounced. Despite a difficult few days, this patrician traditionalist was impressed by Alan's willingness to embrace a Hindu wedding ceremony as well as the planned Christian one. Returning to Wolverhampton, he managed to persuade Mrs Gupta to accept the union.

NICOLA (NIC) HANSON

Borchester • Born 1980

(Becky Wright)

Will Grundy started to go out with the mother of Jake (4) and Mia (2) in the summer of 2007. Having given up her job at Regal Coaches in **Hollerton**, Nic was struggling on benefits with only erratic support from her former partner Andrew. Caring Will soon asked her to move in with him. But the isolation of living in **Casa Nueva** – and the difficulty of being *in loco parentis* on the regular visits of Will's son **George** – proved hard for Nic. Things came to a head when Will accused her of abuse after he caught her smacking George, although in Nic's defence it was after a tussle between George and Mia. Outraged, Nic flounced back to her mum's in **Borchester**, leaving regretful Will wondering what might have been.

BUNTY AND REG HEBDEN

Bunty born 20.2.22
(Bunty – Sheila Allen)

Alistair Lloyd is in the unfortunate position of having an extra set of quasi in-laws – the grandparents of his adopted son **Daniel Hebden Lloyd**. Retired solicitor Reg and wife Bunty are the parents of **Shula**'s first husband Mark. Having had a bad experience in private education as a child, Alistair insisted that Daniel should go to the local state primary, against Reg and Bunty's wishes. But they won the second – and arguably most significant – round, siding with Shula and funding the boy through **Felpersham** Cathedral School since 2006.

HOLLERTON

Yes. I remember Hollerton —
The name, because one afternoon
(No seat!) the London train drew up there
Abruptly. It was late June.
The iPods hissed. Someone cleared his email.
No one left and no one came
On the bare platform. What I saw
Was Hollerton – only the name
*And '**Ambridge** – 6 miles', and grass,*
And Hassett Hills, and silage clamp,
And 'Services to Birmingham – Platform 2.
Wheelchair access via ramp.'
And for that minute a moped growled
Close by, and round him, noisier,
Farther and further, all the cars
*Of **Borchester** and **Borsetshire**.*

With apologies to Edward Thomas

HOME FARM

STOCK

280 ewes (early lambing) • 110 hinds, stags, calves

CROPS

1,124 acres cereals • 148 acres grassland
152 acres oil seed rape • 36 acres linseed
80 acres woodland • 10 acres willow (game cover)
4 acres strawberries • 6 acres maize

OTHER

25-acre riding course • Fishing lake • Maize maze

LABOUR

Adam Macy (managing) • **Debbie Aldridge** (managing)
Andy, Jeff (general workers) • **Brian Aldridge** (relief)
Tom Archer, **Jazzer** (pigs)
William Grundy (gamekeeper), Pete (acting)
Students and seasonal labour • Fly (sheepdog)

With 1,585 mainly arable acres, Home Farm is the largest in **Ambridge** and carries out contract farming for **Brookfield**, the **Estate** and other local farms. As a partner in the Hassett Hills Meat Company, it raises and supplies high quality lamb to butchers and caterers, and sells its venison and strawberries at local farmers' markets.

CLIVE HORROBIN

A guest of Her Majesty • Born 9.11.72
(Alex Jones)

Many families have a black sheep. But when the family in question is the **Horrobins** then it gives a new dimension to the concept. Clive isn't prejudiced – he'll rob anyone, anywhere – but many of his illegal activities have been in the **Ambridge** area. These include an armed robbery on the **Village Shop**, after which he forced his big sister **Susan Carter** to harbour him (for which she served time); a string of burglaries on local homes; and – worst of all – a vicious vendetta against former policeman George Barford, which culminated in 2004 in a firebomb attack on George's house. Badly burned, Clive sought refuge with Susan once more but this time she did the right thing. Clive got 12 years.

THE HORROBINS

6, The Green, and elsewhere

Some think the Horrobins' role in life is to make the **Grundys** look classy. They've certainly had a higher proportion of jailbirds: **Clive**, Keith and **Susan** (now **Carter**) have all done time, and while many felt that Susan's sentence was unwarranted, there was no such sympathy for her brothers. Unfortunate paterfamilias Bert Horrobin is a former road worker and his wife Ivy supplements her pension with cleaning work. Daughter Tracy flits from job to job and it's best not to ask how Gary and Stewart earn their beer money. Perhaps unsurprisingly, **Neil Carter** feels that 6, The Green isn't an ideal environment for the care of his grandson **George Grundy**, no matter how convenient it is occasionally for **Emma**.

MAURICE HORTON

Borchester

(Philip Fox)

A grumpy man with a cleaver in his hand is perhaps not the most reassuring of figures but butcher Maurice has much to be grumpy about. Having lost his wife, son and a previous business through compulsive gambling, Maurice was happy to give up a tottering one-man shop in **Felpersham** to work part-time at the business units at Sawyer's Farm. There he makes sausages for **Tom Archer**, supplementing this with work in a supermarket and butchering the occasional venison carcass for **Home Farm**. Despite Maurice's moody demeanour, **Alistair Lloyd** has much to be grateful to Maurice for. In fact, we'd say Alistair's in his debt, but that might be rather misleading, as Maurice is Alistair's sponsor at the **Borchester** branch of Gamblers Anonymous.

IZZY

Meadow Rise, Borchester • Born 1993
(Lizzie Wofford)

While **Ruth** and **David Archer** found it hard to adjust to daughter **Pip** actually going out with boys, they are both very comfortable with Pip's best friend from **Borchester** Green school. It wasn't always the case, though. There was a country-meets-town culture shock as they slowly saw through Izzy's hooped earrings and crop tops to the funny, generous girl with a talent for music. And Izzy had her own adjustment to make in 2007, when Pip persuaded her to join Young Farmers. Stepfather Dom is not only very taciturn but not a great earner, so Izzy's mum Karen works on a supermarket check-out and has two cleaning jobs to provide for the family, which includes 'mental' (Izzy's description) elder brother Keifer, younger half-sister Minnie and Ghengis the Alsatian.

JAXX CAFF

Borchester

The ubiquitous coffee shop chains have introduced many Britons to the words 'skinny latte' (along with 'two pounds thirty for a cup of coffee?' and 'daylight robbery'). But most **Borchester** residents are happier with **Underwoods**' coffee shop and its consciously retro rival Jaxx Caff. To a soundtrack of 1950s pop classics, manager **Kenton Archer** and Frank the chef offer shoppers and local workers light meals and welcome refreshment. **Emma Grundy** and Polish waitress Otylia (Ottie) help part-time. But when Kenton is your boss that usually means you run the place.

JAZZER

Meadow Rise, Borchester • Born 1984

(Ryan Kelly)

Jack 'Jazzer' McCreary had a feral adolescence, featuring activities such as joyriding, housebreaking and cannabis growing, often in the company of **Ed Grundy**. Jazzer's still no stranger to drugs, despite a bad experience with ketamine which left him a little clumsy and with memory problems. But in recent years he's knuckled down to early starts as a milkman on **Mike Tucker**'s round – and then onto his other part-time job looking after **Tom Archer**'s pigs. Jazzer likes to live life to the full, preferably with a cute girl on his arm. He has been known to arrive at Mike's cold store straight from a club. Careful with that milk van, Jazzer…

SATYA KHANNA

Wolverhampton
(Jamila Massey)

Usha Franks's parents didn't want their daughter to move to the countryside, so for many years Auntie Satya was Usha's main link to the parental generation. Satya often used to descend when she sensed that Usha needed support, even if Usha didn't want it at the time – although the accompanying food parcels were always welcome, as Usha isn't a great cook. After numerous failed matchmaking attempts, you'd think Satya would have been pleased when Usha fell in love with a prominent, pious and professional man. Unfortunately that man was **Alan Franks**, the local vicar, which didn't go down at all well with this devout Hindu. Satya strongly opposed the wedding, until threats to Usha from within the Asian community aroused her protective nature. She became the prime mover in the Hindu end of Usha and Alan's wedding ceremonies, in August 2008.

MARSHALL LATHAM

At Christmas 2007 **Debbie Aldridge** surprised her parents with the news that she had a boyfriend. Like Debbie, Marshall is a British farm manager running a UK-owned farm in Hungary but, unlike Debbie's enterprise, which has a large dairy herd, his is totally arable. Also unlike Debbie, Marshall is a first-generation farmer: his family have no agricultural background. **Jennifer** was desperate to meet the new man, who was described as looking like a young Tom Jones. But while Debbie was happy to spend time with Marshall's family in Hitchin, Hertfordshire, she was more reluctant to introduce him to the cauldron of dysfunction that is the **Aldridge** family.

ALISTAIR LLOYD

The Stables
(Michael Lumsden)

Few people are aware of the angst behind the outward life of busy vet and **Ambridge** cricket captain Alistair Lloyd. He now attends regular Gamblers Anonymous meetings after a period of compulsive poker playing which lost him £100,000 – much of it to **Matt Crawford**. Alistair didn't try to duck his personal responsibility, but his wife **Shula Hebden Lloyd** had to accept that her controlling nature – and the suffocating embrace of the ubiquitous **Archer** clan – had contributed to Alistair's quest for excitement. Taking out a mortgage to pay his debts, Alistair refocused on his practice (which is based at Shula's riding stables) and his relationship with adopted son **Daniel**.

DANIEL HEBDEN LLOYD

The Stables • Born 14.11.94

(Dominic Davies)

In times past, the son of **Shula Hebden Lloyd** and (by adoption) **Alistair Lloyd** was known to some listeners as 'Fat Dan' (no relation to **Fat Paul**). Steroid treatment for juvenile arthritis did indeed make Daniel a junior Michelin Man for a while. Fortunately the condition has been in remission for many years, allowing the boy to participate in his parents' favourite pastimes of cricket and horse riding. In 2006, against Alistair's wishes, Daniel started as a day boy at **Felpersham** Cathedral School, funded by his grandparents **Bunty and Reg Hebden** (Daniel's biological father was Shula's first husband Mark Hebden, who tragically died in a car crash without knowing that Shula was pregnant). It looks as if 'Formerly Fat Dan' may have inherited the Archer farming genes: he often helps **Neil Carter** with his pigs. In 2008, he became a keen star watcher with grandfather **Phil**.

JIM LLOYD

Melrose, Scotland
(John Rowe)

Alistair **Lloyd**'s father is a retired history professor. He's used to fawning acolytes, whether from his old university days or the sea cruises in which his erudite lectures are part of the on-board entertainment. When he's the centre of attention he's absolutely charming, but when he's not he tends to behave badly. This militant atheist nearly drove **Shula** loopy when he moved into **The Stables** to recover from a broken leg over Christmas 2007. **Daniel** loved having Jim around, as he encouraged the lad to challenge his parents' assumptions (and the present of an air rifle might have helped, too). Alistair had to overcome decades of parental subjugation to tell Jim it was time to return to Scotland. Jim left under protest, but not before turning the head of **Ruth Archer**'s mother **Heather Pritchard**.

SHULA HEBDEN LLOYD

(formally Hebden, née Archer)
The Stables • Born 8.8.58
(Judy Bennett)

Shula is still reaping the effects of her out-of-character affair with **Usha Franks**'s former partner Richard Locke in 1998. Ten years later Shula had to resign as churchwarden following unwise remarks to a reporter about Usha's planned marriage to vicar **Alan Franks**. Shula remained a churchgoer and bell-ringer, but her reputation as the solid twin to flaky **Kenton Archer** took another blow in the family. Shula runs a riding school and stables (named, with breathtaking imagination, **The Stables**) and is married to **Alistair Lloyd**. Her first husband Mark was killed in a car crash in 1994, unaware that after infertility treatment Shula was pregnant with **Daniel**.

LOWER LOXLEY HALL

'A great day out for all the family!' claim the flyers and indeed this impressive mansion with extensive parkland has much to offer; quite a lot of it spawned by the passing enthusiasms of its owner **Nigel Pargetter** (one of the reasons his wife **Elizabeth** indulges them). Nigel runs falconry courses and displays with falconer Jessica; the grounds boast rare breeds, cycle trails, an art gallery, a tree-top walk and vines producing Lower Loxley's own wine. He's also a keen horseman; the annual point-to-point was supplemented in 2008 by a gung-ho team chase. And with its more sober hat on, Lower Loxley welcomes conferences, weddings and other functions – especially with a 'green' tinge. Staff include ancient retainers **Edgar and Eileen Titcombe**, volunteer guide **Bert Fry**, retail and catering manager Lorna and Hugh the Orangery Café's chef. **Hayley Tucker** nannies for **Lily and Freddie**, and runs activity visits for schoolchildren.

ADAM MACY

Honeysuckle Cottage • Born 22.6.67

(Andrew Wincott)

When unmarried **Jennifer** (now **Aldridge**) first became pregnant, she refused to name the father, although Adam's shock of red hair implicated local cowman Paddy Redmond. Jennifer's first husband Roger Travers-Macy later adopted the boy. After graduating in agricultural economics, Adam worked on farming development projects in Africa, returning to **Ambridge** in 2003. Despite his successful innovations at **Home Farm**, including a thriving soft-fruit business and an annual maize maze, he's had an uneasy relationship with step-father **Brian Aldridge**. Brian would deny it, but he has difficulties with Adam being gay (Adam is in a civil partnership with **Grey Gables** chef **Ian Craig**). In 2008, under severe threats from Jennifer, who feared her children would lose out to Brian's lovechild **Ruairi Donovan**, Brian made Adam and his half-sister **Debbie** joint managers of the farm, with a generous profit share, and Adam was able to prove his worth.

KATE MADIKANE

(née Aldridge)
Johannesburg • Born 30.9.77
(Kellie Bright)

At the height of Kate's wild teenage days (expelled from school, stealing from home, disappearing with travellers...) **Brian** and **Jennifer Aldridge** must have despaired that their daughter would ever settle down into respectable domesticity. But she eventually did, although it was in Johannesburg with a black South African (**Lucas**), rather than in Edgeley with a nice Young Farmer. Kate has three children, but her eldest **Phoebe Aldridge** lives with Phoebe's father **Roy Tucker** and his wife **Hayley**. Kate's children with Lucas are daughter Noluthando (born 2001) and son Sipho (born 2007). She works as a volunteer in an AIDS orphanage and makes occasional visits back to the scene of her earlier crimes in **Ambridge**. Thankfully things are much less stressful nowadays.

LUCAS MADIKANE

Johannesburg • Born 1972

(Connie M'Gadzah)

Cynics would say that **Kate** getting pregnant by a black South African was just another ploy to shock the more conservative elements in **Ambridge** (it certainly didn't go down well with her grandmother **Peggy Woolley**). But the match has proved a lasting one, even surviving their move from the pleasant surroundings of Cape Town to the more challenging environment of Johannesburg, when journalist Lucas took a job with the South African Broadcasting Corporation. Lucas married Kate in June 2001 and has been a calming influence on her ever since.

KIRSTY MILLER

Borchester

(Anabelle Dowler)

Chirpy Kirsty hasn't been desperately lucky with men in recent years. Her six-year on-off relationship with **Tom Archer** ended in 2005 when he fell for someone else – only for Tom to be dumped himself soon after he'd given Kirsty the 'big E'. While Tom eventually found happiness with Kirsty's best mate **Brenda Tucker**, Kirsty took up with the **Brookfield** herdsman Sam Batton – only to hear the 'it's not you, it's me' speech once again. (Sam was right, it was him: he'd fallen in love with **Ruth Archer** – but that's another kettle of rancid fish.) At least Kirsty didn't let the break-up with Tom sour her job at the family's shop **Ambridge Organics**, where she works for Tom's sister **Helen**. Tom and Kirsty have managed to bury their past and are on good terms now when they meet at the shop or when she's working part-time at **The Bull**.

ELIZABETH PARGETTER

(née Archer)
Lower Loxley Hall • Born 21.4.67
(Alison Dowling)

Elizabeth might be the youngest of **Phil** and **Jill Archer**'s children but my goodness she can punch above her weight, especially when she thinks she's getting less than her fair share. Husband **Nigel** can sometimes be embarrassed by 'Lizzie's' doggedness, but **Lower Loxley** has undoubtedly benefited from the combination of his old-world eccentricity and her pugilistic nature. Before her marriage to Nigel, Elizabeth had an abortion after being dumped by swindler Cameron Fraser. And her congenital heart problem required a valve-replacement operation after the birth of the twins **Lily and Freddie**. Probably as well she's such a fighter.

LILY AND FREDDIE PARGETTER

Lower Loxley Hall • Born 12.12.99

(Theodore and Madelaine Wakelin)

W hen **Elizabeth** was pregnant with twins the family feared for her life, as she was suffering the effects of a congenital heart condition. But Lily and Freddie were born – in that order – safely if a little early by caesarean section. When not on maternity leave, **Hayley Tucker**, once their full-time nanny, still does the school run to and from Loxley Barratt Primary and looks after them in the holidays.

NIGEL PARGETTER

Lower Loxley Hall • Born 8.6.59

(Graham Seed)

Nigel has more fads than a Japanese fashion victim, but most of them have in some way added to the **Lower Loxley** visitor experience. Recent crazes included raising vines to make Lower Loxley wine, restoring a ha-ha and building a memorial to his eccentric great-uncle Rupert (from whom Nigel perhaps inherited his idiosyncratic charm). Increasing concern for the future we're bequeathing to our children (in his case to **Lily and Freddie**) led to Nigel forsaking his car and developing the Hall as an environmentally friendly stately home, insulated with sheep's wool (no, really) and offering 'green' weddings. It's just as well that Nigel has as his wife and co-manager the more pragmatic **Elizabeth**. His heart and her head combine to make Lower Loxley the success it is.

JAMIE PERKS

April Cottage • Born 20.7.95
(Ben Ratley)

Jamie lives with his mother **Kathy** and her boyfriend **Kenton Archer**, although being close (geographically and personally) to his father **Sid** he spends time regularly at **The Bull**, too. Don't worry – Sid's the landlord there. Jamie's in the same year as **Daniel Hebden Lloyd**, although at different schools, so when they play together (if 13-year-olds still 'play') it's usually in **Ambridge**.

JOLENE PERKS

(née Rogers)
The Bull
(Buffy Davis)

When **Fallon Rogers** went on tour with her band in 2008, she had plenty of advice from her mum Jolene. And unlike most mums in this situation, Jolene knew whereof she spoke, after a long career in the British country music scene. A pianist and singer, she wisely dropped her real name (Doreen) and was often billed as the Lily of Layton Cross. But since her affair with and subsequent marriage to **Sid**, it's to **The Bull** that Jolene has devoted her warm personality and generous 'assets' (as the cheaper tabloids have it). Much of the pub's success in recent years has been down to her, with line-dancing sessions, music nights and innovations including a cyber-area with internet access.

KATHY PERKS

(formerly Holland)
April Cottage • Born 30.1.53
(Hedli Niklaus)

2008 brought back a terrible trauma for Kathy, as she gave evidence against former colleague Gareth Taylor, who had raped her at Christmas 2004. To her immense relief, Taylor was sentenced to 15 years for that and another rape. Feeling the need for a fresh start, Kathy resigned her post as retail and catering manager at **Lower Loxley** and took a job running the bar and catering operation at **Ambridge** golf club. Her previous experience at Lower Loxley as a home economics teacher and at **The Bull**, before her divorce from **Sid**, stood her in good stead in her new role. Kathy says she couldn't have got through her ordeal without the support of her partner **Kenton Archer** and (although he didn't know the details) her son **Jamie**.

SID PERKS

The Bull • Born 9.6.44

(Alan Devereux)

Sid Perks is the nicest homophobe you could ever hope to meet. He runs **The Bull**, in which he has a 49 per cent share (with **Lilian Bellamy**), and is married to voluptuous **Jolene**. Sid's first wife Polly died in 1982. Their daughter Lucy and grandson Matt live in New Zealand while **Jamie** – his son from his second marriage – lives in **Ambridge** with **Kathy**. A keen cricketer for most of his life, Sid coaches at Loxley Barratt Primary and still takes an interest in the Ambridge team, despite his distaste at the gay **Adam Macy** being their star batsman. He was a driving force in the team's attempt at the Village Cup in 2007, and qualified as an umpire in the same year.

HEATHER PRITCHARD

Prudhoe, Northumberland

(Joyce Gibbs)

Once a mother, always a mother, but the distance from **Borsetshire** to Northumberland means that **Ruth Archer** doesn't get as much hands-on mothering as Heather would probably like. Widowed since 2002, Heather has a thriving social life and is quite comfortably off, as can be deduced from the number of cruises she takes. It's an interest she shares with relatively new-found friend **Jim Lloyd**, father of Ruth's brother-in-law **Alistair**. (What relation is that, we wonder? Father-in-law-in-law?)

ROBERT PULLEN

Manorfield Close • Born 13.7.15

A resident of Ambridge's little plot of 'old people's homes', Bob Pullen is the son of a Black Country draper. He has many tales about the acts that he saw at Dudley Hippodrome as a young man, although little is known about the intervening decades. He's still a game old bird. Despite his notoriously weak bladder, in 2006 he turned out for the 80th birthday celebrations of that youngster, HM the Queen, and he is always up for an outing with **Ambridge**'s Over-60s Club.

THE STABLES

Located just outside the centre of **Ambridge**, The Stables is the home and business of **Shula Hebden Lloyd**, who bought it in 2001 from her aunt **Christine Barford**. As well as stables offering the usual range of full, half or DIY livery, there's also a riding school complete with indoor arena. Shula's husband **Alistair Lloyd** has his veterinary surgery on site.

FALLON ROGERS

The Bull • Born 19.6.85
(Joanna van Kampen)

After several years trying to make it in the music business, this guitarist and singer took a big step forward in 2008, when her indie band Little White Lies supported a bigger act on a national tour. It was a great experience but sadly it also exposed the weaknesses in her relationship with **Ed Grundy**. Fallon was wise enough to let Ed return to his true love **Emma Grundy** while Fallon returned to **The Bull**, where she lives with mother **Jolene** and stepfather **Sid Perks**. She returned also to her other musical activities, acting as musical director for local shows and promoting music nights in the function room 'Upstairs@The Bull'. And waiting for the phone to ring with that next step to musical stardom, of course.

RONNIE

Farriers make a good living and are often popular with the ladies. We're not sure whether it was this or an interest in horse anatomy and metalworking which drew **Christopher Carter** to the profession. But in 2004 he managed to persuade Ronnie to take him onto the farrier's apprenticeship scheme. Ronnie's faith was justified in 2008 when Chris passed successfully – with only a few wobbles along the way.

GRAHAM RYDER

Borchester
(Malcolm McKee)

As a land agent working for the **Borchester** firm of Rodway and Watson, Graham used to supervise the management of the **Estate**'s 'in-hand' farmland. He was less than gruntled when **Matt Crawford** passed that role to **Debbie Aldridge** in 2006, leaving Graham with little more than collecting the quarterly rent from **Bridge Farm** – and even that task was under threat as **Pat** and **Tony Archer** made moves to buy their freehold. Graham can't quite understand why he is so unpopular in **Ambridge**. He sees himself as courteous and conscientious but others interpret that as oily and nit-picking. It's no wonder he wasn't elected to the parish council when he stood in 2003. The fact that he was widely regarded as Matt's placeman didn't help, either.

ST STEPHEN'S CHURCH

Established 1281

2008 saw some changes in the management of **Ambridge**'s fine parish church, whose history can be traced back to Saxon times. Long-serving churchwardens **Shula Hebden Lloyd** and **Bert Fry** were replaced by **Christine Barford** and **Neil Carter**, who is also captain of the bell-ringers. Bert's replacement was routine but Shula left under a cloud over the controversial marriage of vicar **Alan** and **Usha Franks**. Organist **Phil Archer** has seen many controversies come and go over the years – the installation of a lavatory, the appointment of a woman vicar, the proposed scrapping of the pews... He just kept his head down and his hands on the keyboard.

ANNABELLE SCHRIVENER

Felpersham
(Julia Hills)

With beauty and brains combined, this is one formidable package. Annabelle is senior partner of her own law firm, specialising in property. Having advised **Borchester Land** as a client for some time, in 2007 Annabelle joined the board of the company. It was a typically shrewd business move by BL chairman **Matt Crawford** but not the cleverest from a personal viewpoint, as a flirtation soon developed which threatened his relationship with **Lilian Bellamy**. Annabelle quickly made it clear she wasn't interested in anything serious, and returned to finessing property deals for Borchester Land and Matt himself. As BL's nominated directors, she and Matt also shook up the cosy family arrangements surrounding the planned anaerobic digester at **Home Farm**.

SILENT CHARACTERS

One of the delights of **Ambridge** is that coterie of characters whom the listener knows well and can picture clearly but who are never actually heard to speak. A large but obviously rather quiet band, they include the ageing Mrs Potter and **Mr Pullen** at Manorfield Close; **Lower Loxley**'s gardener **Edgar Titcombe**, housekeeper **Eileen Titcombe**, retail manager Lorna, resident falconer Jessica, chef Hugh and greenwoodworker Alec; **Eddie Grundy**'s friends **Baggy** and **Fat Paul**; **Home Farm** workers Andy and Jeff; **William Grundy**'s deputy Pete; **Bridge Farm** dairy worker Colin Kennedy; exotic Anja at **Ambridge Organics**; waitress Ottie and Frank who flips the burgers at **Jaxx Caff**; bell-ringer **Neville Booth** and his unpopular nephew **Nathan**; **Ambridge Golf Club**'s director of golf Leigh Barham; **Bert Fry**'s ploughing rival Jimmy Prentice; parish council chair **Derek Fletcher**; many of the **Horrobins;** and that latter-day femme fatale **Freda Fry**.

LYNDA SNELL

Ambridge Hall • Born 29.5.47
(Carole Boyd)

The years since Lynda and husband **Robert** arrived from Sunningdale in 1986 have seen a reduction in their circumstances but no diminution of Lynda's indomitable spirit. As Robert lost first his software business and then his career in IT altogether, Lynda started a job as receptionist at **Grey Gables** and later took in B&B guests at **Ambridge Hall**. All this while directing amateur dramatics, crusading on behalf of the environment (often to the irritation of the **Grundys** and local farmers), tending her garden (despite her annual hayfever) and caring for her pet llamas. The fact that they are named Wolfgang, Constanza and Salieri probably tells you all you need to know…

ROBERT SNELL

Ambridge Hall • Born 5.4.43

(Graham Blockey)

Retrenching after the collapse of his software business in 1995, Robert made a decent living with a few small clients and agency work. But when a contract was terminated in 2006 he started to despair of finding another job in the IT industry. To his – and most of his neighbours' – surprise, he found a late-late second career as **Ambridge**'s genial odd-job man. And in 2007 he became chief cook and guest-greeter when he and Lynda started to take in B&B guests. Genuinely in love with **Lynda** (he'd have to be), Robert has two daughters from his first marriage. The younger Coriander ('Cas') is a welcome occasional visitor to **Ambridge Hall**, while Leonie is more of the 'batten down the hatches' type.

CAROLINE STERLING

(née Bone, formerly Pemberton)
Grange Farm • Born 3.4.55
(Sara Coward)

An aristocratic bloom in the nettle patch that is **Ambridge**, Caroline found success in work – managing **Grey Gables** hotel – while suffering serial failure in love. She once had an affair with **Brian Aldridge**, although that hardly makes her unique among **Borsetshire** women, and her (eventual) first husband Guy Pemberton tragically died after only six months of marriage. But latter years have brought greater happiness, with marriage in 2006 to fellow hunting enthusiast **Oliver Sterling** and their purchase of Grey Gables from former owner **Jack Woolley**.

OLIVER STERLING

Grange Farm

(Michael Cochrane)

When Oliver arrived in **Ambridge**, after a divorce and the sale of his large farm in North **Borsetshire**, he was set for a gentle semi-retirement at **Grange Farm**, with a little hobby farming on 50 acres there. But, as joint master of the South Borsetshire Hunt, he met and fell in love with **Caroline**. They were married in 2006 and along the way became joint owners of **Grey Gables** hotel. This apparently conservative, establishment figure proved to be a late-flowering radical, defying industry norms with a small herd of Guernseys supplying **Mike Tucker**'s milk round. He was radical too in placing his trust in herd manager **Ed Grundy**. But when TB attacked the herd in 2008, Oliver came to regret his boldness in producing an unpasteurised cheese, Sterling Gold. Only Ed's entreaties persuaded Oliver to tough it out.

MABEL THOMPSON

Bradford

(Mona Hammond)

The mother of **Alan Franks**' deceased first wife Catherine, Mabel is originally from Jamaica but a long-term resident of Bradford. She's a woman of strong views and her visits to Ambridge can often be lively, to say the least. But although they've previously been able to agree to differ on controversial topics, Alan's engagement and subsequent marriage to the Hindu **Usha** (née Gupta) was simply too heretical for this evangelical Christian. Not only did it drive a wedge between Mabel and Alan, but it soured her relationship with granddaughter **Amy**, too.

SABRINA AND RICHARD THWAITE

Grange Spinney

Well-heeled occupants of one of the most expensive developments in **Ambridge**. Richard commutes to work but finds time to turn out for the Ambridge cricket team. Sabrina is a super-fit 'yummy mummy', whose appearances at village events from pancake races to pub quizzes prove her to be fiercely competitive. She terrifies the life out of **Robert Snell**.

EDGAR AND EILEEN TITCOMBE

Lower Loxley

Who knew that such a bond was developing between the **Pargetters**' head gardener and their housekeeper (formerly Mrs Pugsley), previously noted mainly for their **silent** devotion to their duties. Following the death of Mrs Pugsley's long-estranged husband, Edgar Titcombe was thrown into teen-like torments until, encouraged by **Nigel**, he plucked up the courage to propose to the woman he had worshipped wordlessly for so long. They were married in 2006.

ABIGAIL (ABBIE) TUCKER

Willow Farm • Born 7.3.08

Hayley and **Roy Tucker**'s joy at the prospect of at last having their own child together turned to deep anxiety when Hayley went into labour ten weeks early. But after an extensive period in an incubator and on oxygen, little Abbie developed fully and they were able to bring her home to **Willow Farm**, a much-awaited little sister for **Phoebe Aldridge**.

BRENDA TUCKER

1, The Green • Born 21.1.81

(Amy Shindler)

Daughter of **Mike Tucker** and younger sister of **Roy**. In 2005, frustrated Brenda chucked in her job at Radio **Borsetshire**. But her plans to improve her career prospects by taking a degree were set back by the death of her mother Betty. Getting a taste for commercial life through her involvement with boyfriend **Tom Archer**'s sausage business, she enrolled at **Felpersham** University in autumn 2006 to study marketing. She supplemented her student loan by working for Tom and at **Jaxx Caff**, until **Matt Crawford** spotted her potential and offered her vacation work, Alan Sugar-style, as his apprentice. As Brenda had previously tried to unveil Matt's role in a dodgy property deal and had been dumped by James Bellamy, son of Matt's paramour **Lilian**, this was a characteristically bold Crawford move.

HAYLEY TUCKER

(née Jordan)
Willow Farm • Born 1.5.77
(Lorraine Coady)

2008 saw some big changes in the life of this bubbly and attractive Brummie. Following extended fertility problems, a long-hoped-for pregnancy resulted in the premature (but ultimately successful) birth of **Abbie**. And after years of trying to get on the local property ladder Hayley and husband **Roy** found their housing problems solved in another way: by funding the conversion of **Willow Farm** into two residences. A qualified nursery nurse, Hayley works at **Lower Loxley** as a nanny and runs activities for visiting school parties there. Despite many years in **Ambridge** she still sees herself as a child of the concrete jungle. So since the death of mother-in-law Betty she's been rather surprised to find herself joint manager of an organic egg enterprise with neighbour **Neil Carter**.

MIKE TUCKER

Willow Cottage • Born 1.12.49
(Terry Molloy)

Mike's had a tough life, so he could be forgiven for displaying a bit of a grumpy side. Made bankrupt as a dairy farmer in 1985, he trained in forestry work, only to lose an eye in an accident. Then, tragically, in 2005 he lost his wife Betty. Children **Roy** and **Brenda** cautiously observed Mike's tentative steps back into the dating scene, but after some knockbacks he decided that he was more comfortable in a platonic relationship with his regular ballroom dancing partner Alison. Mike's slow recovery from his bereavement was helped by **Oliver Sterling**'s plan to supply local milk for local people. Mike took on the processing at **Grange Farm**, buying the milk for his round and employing **Jazzer** to share the deliveries. An outbreak of TB in 2008 threatened the whole business, but Mike and Ed persuaded Oliver to let them take on more of the management burden, stocking extra produce in an attempt to weather the storm.

ROY TUCKER

Willow Farm • Born 2.2.78

(Ian Pepperell)

Be-suited Roy is an efficient and popular deputy to **Caroline Sterling**. But the guests at **Grey Gables** could hardly imagine the colourful past of this capable manager. Once part of the group of racist thugs who terrorised **Usha Franks**, Roy soon came to his senses and buckled down to business studies at **Felpersham** University. But while there he had a daughter, **Phoebe Aldridge**, with **Kate Madikane** and fought for his right to raise the child. He later married **Hayley**, the three of them forming a lovely family, enhanced in 2008 by the arrival of **Abbie**. After Roy's sister **Brenda** withdrew her objections, they took up **Mike**'s solution to the challenge of housing the four of them, by converting **Willow Farm** into two dwellings.

UNDERWOODS

Well Street, Borchester

Underwoods department store –
It's the store with so much more!

Kitchen, bathroom, under stairs,
You'll find the things that you need there.
We have clothes for all of you –
Ladies, gents and children too
And the things to feed them all
In our well-stocked fine food hall.
Looking for a present, fellers?
Try our helpful perfume sellers!

Underwoods department store –
It's the store with so much more.

Advertising jingle (rejected)

THE VILLAGE SHOP

Welcome to a rare remaining example of a declining species. When **Jack Woolley** was divesting all his business interests he couldn't quite bring himself to sell the shop, knowing what an important role it played in the life of **Ambridge**. The manager **Susan Carter** tries to maximise trade, with extended opening hours and DVD rental supplementing the traditional grocery shopping and 'oh, we need a bottle of wine' emergencies. While Susan and her husband **Neil** persuaded **Peggy Woolley** (on Jack's behalf) to refurbish and let out the flat upstairs in search of extra income, the village held its breath over the Government's round of post office closures. They were relieved when it was reprieved, at the expense of neighbouring Penny Hassett. After all, if they had lost the shop, where would they get their daily dose of gossip?

WILLOW FARM

Two words denoting a rather complicated piece of real estate. In 2008, the farmhouse was divided and extended. Willow Farm is home to **Roy Tucker,** Roy's wife **Hayley**, his daughter **Phoebe Aldridge** and their daughter **Abbie Tucker**. The smaller half – Willow Cottage – houses Roy's father **Mike**. Nearby is eight acres owned by **Neil Carter** (the rest of the farm was sold long ago). Neil's land houses his outdoor breeding herd of pigs; an organic free-range egg enterprise, run jointly with Hayley; and Ambridge View – **Susan**'s dream house which Neil self-built with Mike's help.

HAZEL WOOLLEY

California, Camden Town... who knows?
Born 15.2.56
(Annette Badland)

Jack Woolley adopted the daughter of his second wife Valerie in 1972. Hazel claims to work in the film business but no-one seems to know exactly what sort of films. She made one of her mercifully rare visits to **Ambridge** in summer 2005 and only left having failed to persuade Jack to sign **Grey Gables** over to her. **Peggy** loves her dearly, of course...

JACK WOOLLEY

The Lodge, Grey Gables • Born 19.7.19
(Arnold Peters)

Self-made businessman Jack Woolley once bestrode the narrow world of **Ambridge** like a Brummie colossus. But as he lost his faculties to the creeping rot of dementia he was forced to sell his enterprises, including **Grey Gables** hotel, his shares in the *Borchester Echo* newspaper and **Jaxx Caff**. Although he makes regular visits to a day centre, the bulk of Jack's care falls to his (third) wife **Peggy**, who spends much of her life protecting him from the unexpected. Jack's adopted daughter **Hazel** (from his second marriage) visits occasionally, but usually with a not-very-hidden agenda that actually make things worse. To finish in as Shakespearian a vein as we started, sadly Jack has reached second childishness and (nearly) mere oblivion.

PEGGY WOOLLEY

(née Perkins, formerly Archer)
The Lodge, Grey Gables • Born 13.11.24
(June Spencer)

As her mother married two men called Perkins, perhaps Peggy was predestined to marry two men called Jack. The widow of **Phil Archer**'s elder brother, with whom she ran **The Bull** for many years, married the wealthy **Jack Woolley** in 1991. Of a conservative bent in many ways, she is very comfortably off in her retirement, but unfortunately her latter years have been blighted by her second Jack's decline due to Alzheimer's disease. Peggy has dealt with this stoically, as befits a former East Ender (no, not that; this is radio) who lived through the Blitz. And she does have support on hand from her children **Jennifer Aldridge**, **Lilian Bellamy** and **Tony Archer**, when she'll let them help.